AF101462

This Handwriting Notebook Belongs To:

A

A is For

B

B is For

C is For

D is For

E is For

F is For

G is For

H

H is For

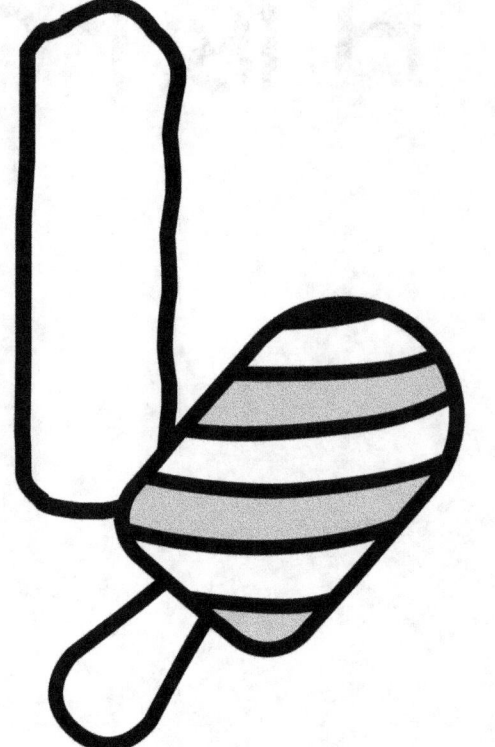

I

I is For

J

J is For

K is For

L

L is For

L is For

M

M is For

N

N is For

O is For

P

P is For

Q is For

R

R is For

s

S is For

T is For

U is For

V is For

W is For

X is For

Y

Y is For

z

Z is For

A Is For Able

B Is For Bright

C Is For Capable

D Is For Delicious

E Is For Exact

F Is For Fair

G Is For Graceful

H Is For Happy

I Is For Ideal

J Is For Joyful

K Is For Kindly

L Is For Lawful

M Is For Marvelous

N Is For Neat

O Is For Observant

P Is For Pure

Q Is For Quick

R Is For Reasonable

S Is For Saintly

T Is For Thoughtful

U Is For Unafraid

V Is For Vital

W Is For Well

X Is For Xenial

Y Is For Youthful

Z Is For Zestful